My Days with Nonna

by
Amanda Blanda

AuthorHouse™
1663 Liberty Drive
Bloomington, IN 47403
www.authorhouse.com
Phone: 833-262-8899

Because of the dynamic nature of the Internet, any web addresses or links contained in this book may have changed since publication and may no longer be valid. The views expressed in this work are solely those of the author and do not necessarily reflect the views of the publisher, and the publisher hereby disclaims any responsibility for them.

This book is printed on acid-free paper.

ISBN: 978-1-4343-1889-3 (SC)

Library of Congress Control Number: 2007907492

Print information available on the last page.

Published by AuthorHouse 02/04/2021

author HOUSE®

This book is dedicated
to my Nonna,

who selflessly dedicated
her life to me.

Many people have a favorite place:
A place they love to go.

For me that place is Nonna's
because I love her so.

Some days we watch cartoons
and play dress-up together.

Other days we play card games
and talk about the weather.

Sometimes she tells me of faraway places
in a land of make-believe.

Sometimes she takes me to meet new faces
and learn about history.

On Sundays we go to church
and kneel down in the pew.

We say our prayers and give our thanks.
We sing our praises, too!

Some days we visit my Zias
and talk about their trips to Rome.

We make spaghetti and meatballs.
Then we head back home.

Sometimes we go to the grocery store
and buy what we are eating for lunch.

Sometimes we bake biscotti
and chocolate cupcakes by the bunch.

Sometimes we go in her garden
and pick flowers for the vase on her table.

Sometimes we open a coloring book
or she reads me my favorite fable.

On days of rain or snow,
she makes her apple pies.

We watch them rise and have a taste.
Then we rest our eyes.

My days with Nonna are always fun
no matter what we do.

She is my home away from home
and my love for her is true.

I love you, Nonna!

Printed in the United States
By Bookmasters